as it comes

a collection of stories, poetry, and
prose about the journey to remembering
the true self

diamond dominique dorris

Illustrations by Kelly Marie
Book design by Jonnell Chavez

ded·i·ca·tion

this book is dedicated to the tribe
still making peace with their crooked paths.

the tribe that spent more time on their faces
doctoring scraped knees from tripping
over self-sabotage.

the tribe that misplaced their power
or forfeited authority,
never told they had a choice
or a voice.

the tribe that feels
this is their last attempt at life
or gave up because apathy
was a better mask
than fear.

this book is dedicated to all aspects of me;
the resolved and the "healing in progress".
we are in a state of unconditional self-acceptance.

Table of
con·tents

Gratitude
ac·knowl·edg·ments

parents
lover(s)
sister(s)
family and relatives
friends and enemies
you all reminded me
of who i am.

there would be
no story
without you.

to the Creator i chose
to surrender to—
this book belongs to you.

thank you.

reminder

grow for yourself.
you won't feel disappointed
when others don't notice.

1

soul

To whom i love the most *(part one)*,

across your many lifetimes you always found your way back
to me. a seeker of truth, you always made it your purpose to
remember me. what you're searching for is unconditional. it's
an eternal love that is worth waiting for; just like you. because
to me, you're worth being patient for.

i'm here because you asked me to place love notes in the crisp
morning air; in the leaves that dance around your feet in the
fall; in the white noise your fan composes while you sleep
through the warm summer nights; in the laughter of those
you make smile with your sense of humor; in the morning
ballad of the blue birds; in the winter rain you run from; in
the light codes from the sun as it kisses your skin in spring…

in your lovers, friends, and your enemies; in your fits of rage; in your traumas and triggers; and in the pain you unsuccessfully try to hide.

pardon the tinges of crimson and splatters of pink that found residence in this missive i left for you to find. your heart insisted this was the only way you would know i am here—

i am still here anticipating your homecoming.

as another day comes to a close, i want to remind you again: my love surpasses all natural understandings. it can fill all the blunders, bumps, and bruises of what was, what is, and what will come.

one day, every decision you make will reflect how important i am to you. and one day, you will realize my love for you is not an afterthought.

The mission

you won't find home
on this rock.
this place was never meant
for us to stay.

you are here
to support others
while they remember
how to release
their anchors.

Inner dialogue *(part one)*

"do you remember where you are from? if i showed
you who you are, just as i've done before, could you
recognize your own legacy? what are you so afraid
of?"

i'm afraid to know how i feel. i'm afraid what i feel
is wrong. i'm afraid to discover all the desires i may
be incapable of fulfilling. i'm afraid to carry guilt
for past failures. i'm afraid to let go. i'm afraid the
world will know i am a tree that bears no fruit. i
rather have no part in how my life plays out and
spend my days tuned in to a reality that reminds me
i am not fit to be in charge of my own destiny. i'm
afraid that if i fail, i will be reminded that i'm not
worthy of success.

"your determination to experiment with your own
gifts, even at your own expense, says otherwise. we
both can sense your desire to be whole again, but
the thing is, you already are. while you complain
about doing the work, you've done most of it just
by being here and saying how you feel."

degrees

there are levels to grace.

when life throws you overboard
grace can be a life boat
or a life vest.

sometimes grace is
the calm waters
or the strength to swim.

but for you
grace is the protection over your life;
to ride the waves
alone
exposed
unscathed.

and when they ask you
you will say the miracle
was being able to float.

the past repeats itself
when you are determined to change it.

2

re·mem·ber

Latin *rememorari*;
"Recall to mind."

on this journey there will be individuals, entities, and even parts of yourself that are in complete opposition to your growth. there will be resistance to releasing "toxic" behaviors that served you well in the past. you will have to face the fear that if you change your patterns, your needs may not be met.

you may feel insecure, frustrated, and angry with God or yourself. the uncertainty will *feel* like a threat to you. people might call you weak for moving on with your life. some days you'll psych yourself out with thoughts saying it's not okay to be yourself. submerge yourself in that uncomfortable feeling. put it all on the table. what is all this trying to tell you? what does it point to?

the answer must come to you.
you don't have a choice.

some days you will accept this.
your days will flow.

some days you will be anxious.
your days will blur.

don't fix anything.
feel into it.

altar

it's ok to be afraid
and think change
won't work.

if you want a life
with you standing in your way
start a war.

tell yourself
how you feel is wrong.
numb yourself
as you've done before.

if you choose
to call a truce
you must cover your fears
in empathy
and understanding.

thank them for being
part of you
protecting you
alerting you of your limits
and boundaries.

unpacking is a lifetime event of recognizing the conflicts between your thoughts and actions. to know where the mind is, look at what you choose to do. the subconscious is who you think you are the moment you are not paying attention.

Inner dialogue *(part two)*

it took one time to learn that fire will burn me, one year to learn calculus, and one heartbreak to learn not to trust, but i have spent what feels like forever questioning my existence. why is it taking me so long to believe in myself?

"unlearning' is dependent upon the wound, the intensity of trauma, and bandwidth to integrate new information. sometimes you'll struggle with a new concept because you are not done experiencing the old one."

what do i do?

"try on every lifestyle and tailor it to your preferences. you are not bound to any design. you will find a piece of yourself in every label. eventually, you won't want to wear anything. you will know you are perfect as you are."

when you don't know who you are
others shoulder the responsibility to tell you.

and you will wear every opinion
like a second skin
until you remember.

let my life be a reminder of what i am capable of when i allow God to use me...

prayer

Affirmation

i give myself space
patience and grace
to repeat lessons.

sometimes mistakes
are required to grow.

there is no wrong answer
no wrong way and
no wrong time.

i am where i am *meant to be*.

everything is sewn together seamlessly
in favor of my evolution.

all things have worked
are working
and will work together
for my good.

3 Chapter three
grief

Latin *gravare*—
"Make heavy".

at the age of twelve i gave birth to my eldest seed, a
stillborn—

a dream i cut the cord to. asphyxiation by anger. i grew tired
of waiting for change and had no outlet, so i let it out on
myself. it died in my shame thinking it did something wrong. i
lived with the guilt of forfeiting my purpose. many babies i
aborted to hide any signs of weakness. i was so embarrassed
of the mess i made, i wouldn't name them out of fear it would
make things real for me. so in the dead of night i dropped my
issues on the doorsteps of families, friends and strangers then
accused them of child endangerment and neglect. i thought it
would make things easier.

but i still cried at night over my offspring, my broken dreams, all while i continued to destroy their home with criticism.

there were some pregnancies that never showed, others i couldn't hide, and sometimes i was clueless to the signs that i was with child until it was time to push.

i still remember the cravings of love, revenge, redemption— and i was eating for more than two so i chose to walk aside those that didn't cherish me; willing to beg to be fed.

i carried the skeletons of my offspring into adulthood and allowed them to occupy my womb with their lifeless bodies. my temple became septic holding on to them. i just wanted them around to see that i finally learned how to love.

i wish i could've shown them how much they meant to me. i wish they were here to experience the version of me that knows i'm safe to love freely. today i express gratitude for my offspring. they were willing to be my mirror and show me how i treated myself. they were willing to die as my teacher.

as i wipe away the last of yesterday's tears, i find myself worn out by my cries over corpses. i cannot change what has happened. but i can allow myself the opportunity to give my babies the proper send-off if i lay to rest the limiting belief of giving life to dead things. i've decided today is the last day that i lament over the graves of all my unmet expectations.

farewell to all my dreams of how i thought my life should be. i'm calling them all by name so we can both be set free.

i want you to come home. may we all live in peace, and enjoy life *as it comes*.

Spring equinox *(part one)*

to the doormat
hiding behind identities of others
longing for acceptance somewhere
anywhere

explain yourself at your discretion.
you don't have to justify your reason for being.
you don't need a reason to be your first priority.

you deserve a love that won't exploit you.
people will still love you if you put yourself first.
challenge your fear of being alone
by being of service to you.

be who you want to spend the rest of your life with
and the only person you want to live for.
fall in love with your voice.

create boundaries that abide by you
and bring no harm to others.
free yourself from commitments
that ask you to starve yourself to feed others.
love but not at your own expense.

to the manipulator
so afraid of unmet needs

at one point silence meant survival
but things are different now.

you don't have to play games.

let people know what you need.
use your words to take up space.

you can have it if you say so.

deception disgraces you.
it never felt good
you just thought you had to.

you do not need to play victim
to receive love anymore.
there is enough for you.

to the ugly and invisible
that i was too terrified to show
and too ashamed to hide
i was blind to your beauty
and mine
forgive me

your greatest gift to this world
is everything that makes you unique.

accept compliments as a practice.
do not cancel words that
recognize you as the love of God.
don't let anyone show you up
in celebrating you.

you are allowed to receive love
while you are a work in progress.
scars are reminders of wisdom we paid for.
wear them proudly.
you came here to be seen.
promise to forgive yourself
when you forget who you are.

"… loss presents an opportunity to reinvent your life and create a "new normal". death is a rebirth; not just for whatever is in transition, but for the people that are left behind. as we learn how to function in a world without the people or things that once made us feel safe, we are given the obscure opportunity to flow and create a new narrative, or be resistant to the fact that flowing is really the only choice we have…

… loss is your reminder that whatever you lose cannot weaken or reduce the true essence of who you are. having nothing to lean on is a reminder of how powerful you are on your own.

… if the universe is guiding you to carry less, it is because what you are about to receive requires more room in your life…"

— **Excerpt** | *moving forward, learning to absorb the loss*

the practice of forgiveness
comes a few sizes too big
because it is meant
for you to grow into.

4

Chapter four
for·give·ness

From vulgar Latin *perdonare*—
"To give wholeheartedly, to remit."

To whom i love the most *(part two)***,**

there will come a time when you will have to extend
forgiveness towards everyone, including people you would like
to maintain a relationship with. what you've been expecting to
come from your relationships was something only seen in
movies. you asked for something genuine, so get comfortable
with imperfection.

i cannot say you will never be hurt again. that is for you to
decide. more times than not, it is you that hurts you the most.
the best way to maneuver in the real world is to forgive and
not take anything personally. we are all just roleplaying our
stories with one another.

compassion is

putting yourself in someone else's shoes to
understand the decisions that were made. it
is not synonymous with overlooking one's
harmful actions. the pain they caused may
not be personal, but you are not required to
tolerate it. if it does not feel good, feel free
to move on at any time.

compassion,
kindness,
and forgiveness
are not weaknesses
or flaws
just because others
were unable to
accept, express,
and reciprocate
your love.

price

it costs nothing to love.

but love does not mean
i will carry you
endure abuse
or allow you
to bring me harm.

i will accept you as you are
and this can be done from a distance.

forgiveness does not include
access back into my space.

resentment is such a waste of creative energy.

Trust

we were not made to take
karma's place
carrying heaviness
in our hearts to enforce
our level of integrity on others.

it is not our place
and not our concern
to teach them a lesson.

instead of looking back
look to the universe's
self-correcting
restorative superpowers;
the eternal beauty mark
the true power of God.

you are covered.

you are able and you've always been.
forgive yourself if you forgot.
be patient if you can't forgive today.
honor, love, and accept where you are,
wherever you are, anyway.

every critical moment in my life was
a reminder that even when the gun is
pointed at me and the trigger is
pulled, what i feel is the pressure of
my experience, but the bullet *cannot*
kill me *without* my consent.

5

bound·ary

Medieval Latin *bunda*—
"Boundary marker."

love won't ask you to sacrifice
boundaries or relationships.

love doesn't cost respect
or dignity.

love won't ask you to betray yourself.

someone unwilling to love you
is their missed opportunity
not yours.

there are people in this world
you won't have to beg to love you.

Spring equinox *(part two)*

i may not—

be dishonest with myself.
go against my feelings for approval.
put down others to feel good about myself.
put myself down as a punishment.
hold on to what doesn't highlight my truest self.
use my abilities to bring harm to others.
settle for anything less than what is meant for me.
compare myself to anyone else.
neglect my gifts.

people may not—

use me to dump or bypass their emotions.
insinuate that i am worth less.
gossip around me.
lie in front of me or ask me to lie for them.
invade my space without permission.
use my traumas or needs to gain control of me.
use me to bring harm to others.
affect my mood or control how i feel.
negotiate what i am worth.

to protect my energy it is okay to—

change my mind
stand by my decision
cancel a commitment
take a day off
not answer that call
share none of me
share all of me
do nothing
be alone
be with others
sleep in
speak up
stay silent
move forward
step back
step up
say no
let go
hold on
change.

Inner dialogue *part three)*

i am no use to you.

                    "according to you."
nothing about me is 'good'.

                    "according to you."

i'm too loud. i'm stubborn and quick to anger. i
hate how i look. i tend to be impulsive and
defensive. i feel alone. most days it's difficult for
me to focus. i—

    "but i don't find flaws in any of that. focus on
      your timing. everything i gave you is useful."

if it's so useful then why does it work against me?

"you were meant to own it, but no one can make
   you use it correctly. everyone chooses how they
will use their superpowers. the better question is:
  do you think those are flaws, or is that just what
                   everyone told you?"

it is not your job to bridge the gap
between who you are and everyone's
misunderstandings about you. you do
not need them to agree with you on who
you are for what you say to be true.

there's no need to police
the blessings of others.

be *so* full you have no desire to focus
on the plates beside you.

Inner dialogue *(part four)*

can you tell me what a boundary is in a poem?

"wrapped with neutrality
and grace,
proactive and transparent,
with respect for everyone;
accepting responsibility
for the energy it both brings and allows;
it never interferes
with love passing through."

beautiful.

problems i faced in my adult life were a result of me forcing what was never meant to be or resisting changes in my life. i thought having an open heart was a curse because i was easy to deceive, but it wasn't them. it was me refusing to honor my intuition. the soul always knows.

(in)charge

when you take ownership
over your life
behaviors
that don't align
with who you truly are
you can say
you don't want
to keep.

guilt, shame, and fear have no place in my life.

O' vessel of clay

water cannot pour
from an empty cup.

to be full
is to not worry
if you're enough
for everyone else.

only a filled tub can give
water to the floor.

love can only pour
from your overflow.

there is a chance
you may be labeled rude
or out of compliance
because the only desire you will have
is to honor yourself.

you will be labeled defiant
for changing the status quo.
this is a test.

you wanted to know
who loved you for you,
now you are being shown the truth
as you learn to love yourself.

love won't put you in harm's way
but ignoring discernment will.

i am my equilibrium.
this is *self-centered*.

6 Chapter six
un·der·stand

Old English *understanding*—
"Stand in the midst of".

Inner dialogue *(part five)*

i didn't want to let go of what i thought my home
should look like. i was afraid that if i did, i wouldn't
find a love i'm worthy of. i felt the universe didn't
have my best interest at heart so i had to advocate for
myself. today, the home i have now is not the home i
wanted or dreamed of. it's even better. God gave me
something i never knew was possible. my home is
heartfelt. it is here right now.

"go on."

when we can find peace with what we are experiencing, we can live in the moment and find home everywhere. and when we are lonely, it's because we don't remember who we are.

"you really are the light of my life."

i spent my life thus far longing for
acceptance from the same people that
were willfully against seeing me outside
of their own prejudices. i gave so much
time away fighting to be seen, heard,
loved, and for nothing. one thing i know
for sure: being understood is a luxury i
cannot afford.

a radical act—
 repainting the walls of old experiences.

a transformative act—
removing them.

you keep asking for signs, answers, and omens. and i
keep sending them. but somehow you are still
looking. i've told you time and time again, but it is
not the answer you want. what is it that you are still
pretending not to know?

sensual

i never found a label in life
worth identifying with.

i've been liked
loved
owned
kept
possessed
admired
but understood…
not so much.

i never knew how to fit in
and i couldn't explain to others who i was.

it took years to realize
that i am not a category
title
or label

but an experience
too many words can ruin.

i'm not for everybody—
honestly it's better off that way.

exhaustion is a clear indication
you're trying to control things
that are *none* of your concern.

7 Chapter seven
fo·cus

Latin *focus*—
"Hearth, fireplace."

you are not what you attract. life has never been about what you attract. you will meet all kinds of people, and come in contact with all kinds of opportunities. not every experience will be a vibrational match to you, and none of them reflect who you are as a person. anything and anyone in your life is just a sign of your focus and priorities, nothing more.

what do you allow? who are you letting in?

unlearning false beliefs
brings you no closer
to accepting new ones.

shift your focus
from unlearning
to transforming
and your new beliefs
will remove old ones for you.

do not confuse
what is familiar
with what feels good.

it may (or may not) be the life i wanted,
but it will always be the life my decision's chose.

grown

8 Chapter eight
man·i·fest

you, nor God, can fulfill your desires only by knowing what you do *not* want. the universe cannot be clearer than you on what you need. God cannot be more explicit with answers than you are with requests.

this reality responds to what you've prepared yourself for, not just your words.

design your world
to have the capacity
to fit what you're
praying for.

it is the universe's role
to produce
but yours
is to be ready
to walk through doors
you expect to come.

faith works

you are so powerful
you've manifested
every opinion
you believed was true
about yourself since
before you were born.

The art of prayer

our Creator works outside of time, space, choices, pains, and loves. the mistakes you made (and will make) have already been known and accounted for in a dimension where everything will happen, is happening, and has already happened. your needs were met before you reached your mother's womb.

God is not working. God is finished. so why do you come to prayer "asking" as if you have not been answered?

prayer is a practice of looking beyond external circumstances, connecting with Source, surrendering, and helping you learn how to acknowledge, express, and accept what your needs are. prayer is recognition that we cannot, and do not, travel alone. prayer teaches us the art of communication and how to be vulnerable, intimate, and open with the only one that can hear your heart speak.

let wishes
be as elaborate
imaginative
and vivid
as possible.

hold that feeling
then let it go.

forgive what leaves
rejoice for what stays.
you don't need anything
that walked away
to bless you.

steps of an alchemist

the fool begs.

the intellectual never asks twice.

the child of God speaks into form.

the fool resists.

the intellectual redirects.

the child of God is an alchemist.

1. you are safe and free to believe in your own
power; create your own experience.

2. this is a world of infinite possibilities.
you will always find the evidence for what you
believe is true.

"Is it not written in your law, I said, ye are gods?"

John 10:34

Journal excerpt *(part one)*

… i've made the decision to stop telling God i'm not ready when God has already said that *I Am*. if anyone knows what i'm capable of, it would be the one who made me. it's time to rely on that truth.

since you can't stop what's coming
pray for a smooth transition instead.

9

Chapter nine
faith

Latin *fides*—
"To trust."

Journal excerpt *(part two)*

i'm letting go of what i think "everything will be okay" means.
i'm open to "okay" having many positive outcomes, not just
the one i envisioned. i'm willing to give God more creative
control over my life. i really don't care how God gets it done
anymore. the 'how' in my life isn't any of my business.

mountains

faith is explicit in word
thought and deed,
working towards the unseen
aligning to receive.

faith is stillness.
acceptance.
surrender.
allowing.

faith is unspoken and implied.
the confidence in both self and God
to guide us on a path
that reflects our truest essence.

faith is fluid
and open
in storms
of unforeseen
circumstances.
showing up when
needed most.

faith works
within your realm
of expectations.

faith is universal currency,
speaking on our behalf.
already done on earth
as it is in heaven.

what we receive
is not a reflection
of what we are worth
but instead
a reflection
of what *we* think
we are worth.

"time" protects us from ourselves. it is impossible to destroy a destiny we don't have direct access to. this is to our benefit. the blessing is being in communication with "tomorrow" through our actions right now. the test you thought you failed was not meant to prove to everyone else you weren't ready. the test was given to show you what you need to work on so you *can* be ready.

"not yet" is **not** a "no". learn the lesson. stop sulking over what you were expected to lose. there is no rush.

what is in store for you, not even *you* can ruin.

as it comes

prayer is an act;

a process of
word to matter
and gratitude
as you wait
for your harvest.

i am open and ready to accept and receive miracles.

my prayers are always answered.
i welcome the very best in my life.

10 Chapter ten
sur·ren·der

Latin *super* "over" + *reddere—*
"Give back; restore."

note2self

i'm just as scared as you
but let's take the leap anyway.
i have enough faith
for the both of us.

if my petals choose to go
let them fall.

if i were to lose them all
it wouldn't matter.

nothing can change
the fact that i am a flower.

i made those petals on the floor.
i can make more.

crux

Paint + sip

chaos is divine order
beyond our own understanding.

i rejoice when things fall apart.
i daydream about the ways
the universe will use
these obstacles
to exalt me and honor God.

in the meantime—
do not mind the mess.
i'm just mastering
the art of me.

the peace i have now is worth everything i lost.

11

peace

From Latin *pacem* —
"Treaty of tranquility, absence of war."

peace comes with
its own paradigm.

it will not share you with
obsolete thoughts
nor coexist with
antiquated truths.

Inner dialogue *(part six)*

how will i know a story is not *my* story anymore?

"you will know when you're busy listening to
yourself tell a new one."

can you tell me how i will know when something
is meant for me?

"you will know it is meant for you when the path
isn't easy, the road isn't clear, and neither
disturbs your peace."

Heaven's scent

when your perfume is
bliss, the fragrance of
God will always precede
you when you enter a
room and it will linger
when you leave.

Journal excerpt *(part three)*

i thought i would find healing once i knew what to do
with my broken pieces, but the real healing was in
knowing i was never broken. every jagged edge turned
out to be what was needed for me to become the key
that could open doors for others.

12

pur·pose

Old French *porposer* —
"To put forth."

Path

losing your way
then realizing you
were always on your way.

rinse and repeat.

don't just stay the course
learn to love it.

reflection 040116—

as romantic as the concept sounds, my self-love journey thus far has been tiring:

full of lovers that weren't equally yoked, people that did not consider me a priority, denial, self-sabotage, self-blame, and believing i didn't deserve anything that brought joy. it would be fair to think i never loved myself at all after reading this list. what's so romantic about anxiety, anger, sadness, and frustration? it sounds crazy to say that self-love motivated *and* stopped my suicide attempts— that self-love had me looking in wrong places and lifeless things. i had to get my hands and heart dirty to dig deep and be okay with being under construction in public. but this will always be considered my most courageous act of love. all of it guided me back to everything i was resisting to feel. i loved myself enough to trigger myself in areas i needed to work through and release, and i came out strong.

i know to trust when something doesn't feel right, when i'm not okay, or when i need a change. i sunk to a place where i had no choice but to listen, and no one to lean on but myself. i loved myself enough to experience what unhappiness felt like. at times, we need to see what we do not want so that we can know what it is that we do want. nothing else says "i love you" more than that.

the best part about you
is that you are *everything*
i didn't know i could pray for.

i fall in love *all over again*
when i see you in your flow.

i am so in love with myself.
this is what right feels like.

i only *hope* you love yourself
as much as i love me,
because this isn't something
i want to experience alone.

Journal excerpt *(part four)*

today was perfect. it had problems like any other, but i set the rhythm. i savored the moment. i came face-to-face with my reality and i held myself responsible for it. i made the day flow how i wanted it to. i recognized tools and used what i had to make the best choice for myself. i identified emotions without criticism. i rewired limiting thought patterns as they arose. there was no pressure or comparison. just me and God.

these are the days i want to recreate. these are the days i want to live for.

Affirmation

i was created in the perfect eyes of God.

if i am good enough to be here,
who am i not good enough for?

"One of them, an expert in the law, tested him with this question: "Teacher, which is the greatest commandment in the law?" Jesus replied: "'Love the Lord your God with all your heart and with all your soul and with all your mind.' This is the first and greatest commandment. And the second is like it: 'love your neighbor *as yourself*.'"

Matthew 22:34-40

13 Chapter thirteen
love

Journal excerpt *(part five)*

i want to share myself with the world so everyone can see why it was so natural for me to fall in love with myself. i want to love myself in such a way that the only plausible explanation is that there *is* a God....

gas yourself the way you gas the ones
you love. you deserve accolades; an
act of reverence. take this moment to
honor your resolute and unwavering
spirit. you made it this far.

To whom i love the most *(part three)*,

i'm forever here for you. how many ways can i show you that i live for you? i'll do them all. you can lean on me. when you fall, i'll be there to catch you. when you feel lonely, know i'm forever by your side. i will love you on the days you remember me, and i will love you even more on the days you don't. i'm always excited to share my world with you. i'm exceedingly rich with love. i'll always have more than enough to give. i can't get enough of you, so you could never be too much for me.

a conscious choice

i once thought true love was a quixotic, passionate whirlwind with two people who knew exactly how to love each other from the moment they met. this concept of love was easy to idolize because it required no effort. there is no challenge to being in a relationship with someone that thinks just like me.

i find myself more intrigued by the most unlikely, candid connections. connections where two people may not always think the same, or need each other, and still prefer their worlds with each other in them. they wake up and choose each other every day. teaching someone how to love you is a practice of honesty, communication, patience, and vulnerability; the commitment to adjustments as two whole and separate lives collide.

i appreciate anyone willing to be flexible enough to love someone like me; thank you for sticking around in a world that has been made for us to find partners and friends that we don't have to learn to love.

attracting people that love the way i love myself.

Inner dialogue *(part seven)*

"when was the last time you fell in love with someone that you didn't have to protect yourself from?"

when i fell in love with myself.

self-worth has become less
about 'worth' to me,
and more about discovering
the worth of everything
through the love
i have for myself.

deserving has become less
about acquiring resources
for personal gain,
and more about showing myself
as reliable and responsible
with what i was already given.

Greatest hits

i knew the love was real
when i would listen to love songs
and sing them to myself.

a song for you (me)

you *are*
what love feels like,
how it appears,
and exactly what love can do
in and through others.

made in the image of love,
my favorite color,
already everything love
is capable of.

where there is love
there is no power struggle.

Journal excerpt *(part six)*

the most valuable thing anyone can give me is quality time. it's a huge honor to know that out of everyone in this world, someone prefers to spend their time with me. i'm honored to know i was the one they wanted to make their future memories with.

Languages

take the time
to be fluent
in my foreign
tongue.

be aware
of the specificity
of my needs.

the feeling is
confirmation
that i am
heard.

to be clear,
i don't want to complete you.

i want to be complete *with* you
and become undone by our growth.

may we gravitate to those
whose soul desire
is to experience
being whole with us
together.

if you want to be good to me, be good to you.

i prefer to pray in silence
and let my heart speak.

somethings
there aren't enough words
in the world to say.

14

Chapter fourteen
heart

To whom i love the most *(part four)*,

first, i want to let you know that i hear you. second, i want to say thank you for having the courage to write about the storm while you were in it. you thought it would make you less credible. you had so much doubt in how your transparency would be received. but you pushed past yourself because it felt right to share what i told you even when you had the hardest times receiving it. you didn't want others to drown because you were still learning how to save yourself. you wrote despite feeling that you reached your ceiling. some days you felt as if you hadn't grown at all. you didn't want to disappoint others. the words felt so massive to type, but that was so you could live in its shadows; to let your work have a voice of its own. you were not created to hide. it is when you hide that the world needs you the most.

we still need you here
(note2self)

don't rob the world of knowing you
trying to be somebody else.

you don't have to bring a thing
or be anything
other than yourself.

we are still waiting to sit with you.
show up for me please.

you won't be disappointed.

i have a vicious habit
of changing a life
for the better.

do not be ashamed
of emptiness.
it's the perfect
opportunity
to be filled with peace.

if you cannot find
an example
it's because
it is your opportunity
to become one.

To my inner child—

you light up the entire room with your smile and i will do anything i can to keep it on your face until i leave here. i truly live for you. when i'm really hard on myself, i like to look at pictures of you. i can't believe i was once you, and you are now me. when i call myself names and judge myself for not knowing better, i remember that i share a heart with you. i can't imagine telling you the things i tell myself, but i still do when i'm angry or upset. you always forgive me, though. you say you know i'm just doing my best. you still want nothing less than to have the best with me. when i want to end it all, i start over because of you. you deserve to be here. i'll be gentler. kinder. i promise. i'll keep my heart open for the both of us. that's all you ever wanted. every day is a celebration of life. i will treat every day like it's my first; with curiosity, passion and enthusiasm to discover what all is out there.

i got you. i love you more than life itself.

forever, my first and last breath. i appreciate everything you've done to ensure my survival. your sacrifices kept me safe. holding on to old programs of anger didn't benefit either of us in any way, but you were only doing the best you could with the information you had, and the people you knew.

i forgive you for every injury that was a result of your
misinterpretations of the world(s) around us...

you have the highest honor for making sure i arrived as an
adult in one *peace.*

i treasure our blossoming friendship. you're my most valuable
ally; you set aside the fear of vulnerability so we could create
something new within us— something that is suitable for the
new narrative we've chosen to live by.

may we live our remaining days in physical manifestations of
our love. may we rest in incomprehensible, indecipherable,
unexplainable peace. may we keep our hands clean, our hearts
light, and our peace close.

fin.

words from the author

i thank everyone for being the reason i write; thank you
for trusting me to articulate feelings many thought there
were no words to describe. thank you because even
though i wrote this book to myself, you were able to
find me in yourselves just as i found you with my words.
i guess what i'm saying is, we are remembering one
another. we really aren't that different, and we are never
too far to go back home.

twitter and instagram: @lovethediosa
site: lovethediosa.com

72549438R00063

Made in the USA
Columbia, SC
31 August 2019